Christmas Memories for Two

MELODY BOBER

7 Early Intermediate to Intermediate Piano Duet Arrangements of the Season's Most Nostalgic Carols

The Christmas season is filled with wonderful memories from my childhood: the huge Christmas tree at my grandparents' house, homemade holiday treats, the reading of the Christmas story from the Bible, and, of course, Santa's visit!

As I reflect over the years of holiday celebrations, the *music* of the Christmas season remains the highlight. Although traditional carols are wonderful to perform as solos, what could be better than sharing these beautiful melodies with a duet partner?

Christmas Memories for Two is a series that contains some of my favorite carols arranged as duets. Whether these pieces are played by two students, a parent and child, or a teacher and student, my hope is that *together* new and exciting memories of the Christmas season will unfold.

Merry Christmas!

Alfred Music Publishing Co., Inc.
P.O. Box 10003
Van Nuys, CA 91410-0003
alfred.com

ISBN-10: 0-7390-8301-5
ISBN-13: 978-0-7390-8301-7

What Child Is This?

SECONDO

Traditional English melody
Arr. by Melody Bober

What Child Is This?

PRIMO

Traditional English melody
Arr. by Melody Bober

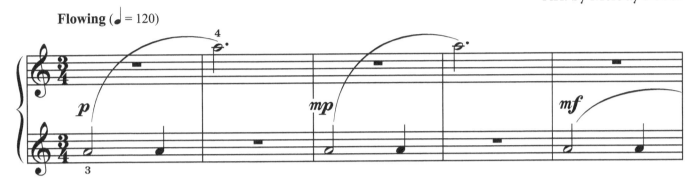

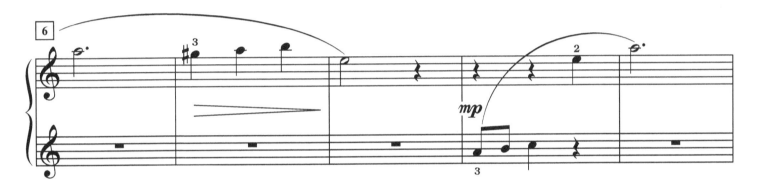

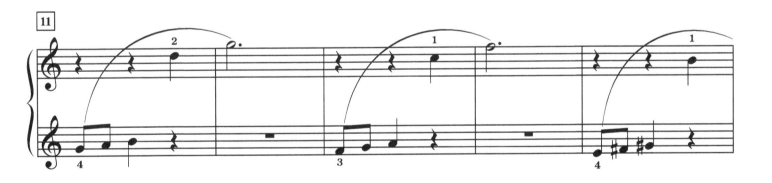

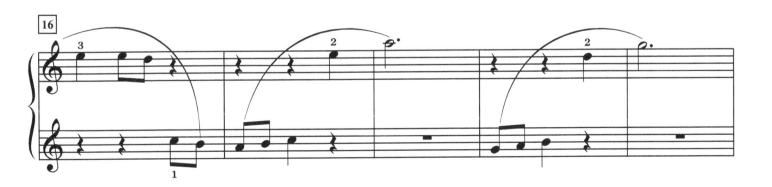

Joy to the World

SECONDO

Lowell Mason
Arr. by Melody Bober

Joy to the World

PRIMO

Lowell Mason
Arr. by Melody Bober

SECONDO

Away in a Manger

SECONDO

James R. Murray
Arr. by Melody Bober

Away in a Manger

PRIMO

James R. Murray
Arr. by Melody Bober

SECONDO

Angels We Have Heard on High

SECONDO

Traditional French melody
Arr. by Melody Bober

Angels We Have Heard on High

PRIMO

Traditional French melody
Arr. by Melody Bober

With excitement (♩ = 126)

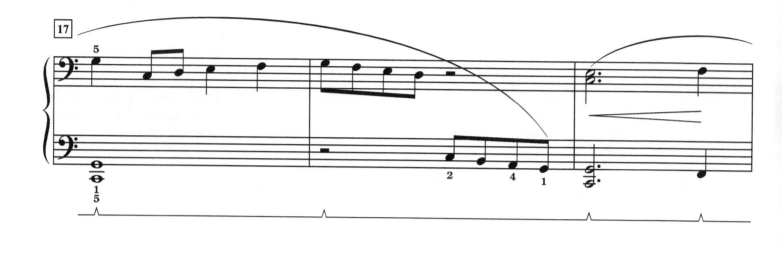

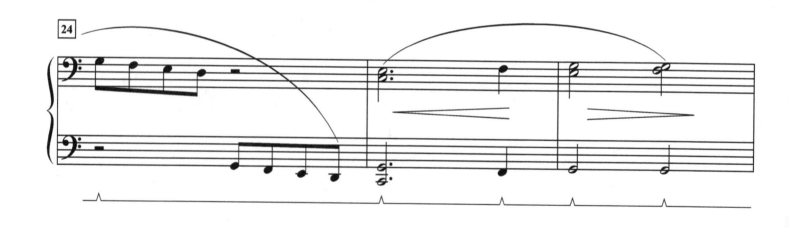

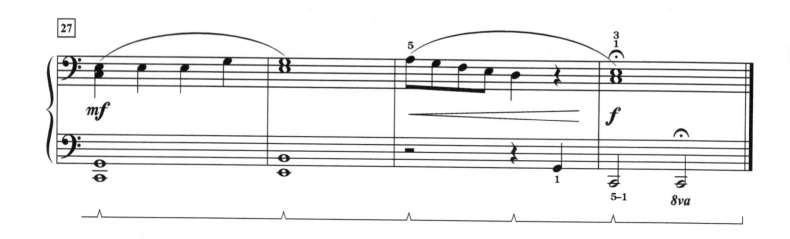

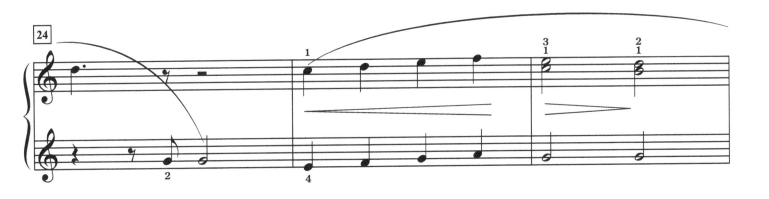

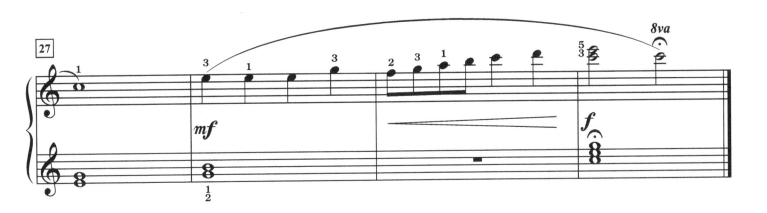

Silent Night

SECONDO

Franz Grüber
Arr. by Melody Bober

Silent Night

PRIMO

Franz Grüber
Arr. by Melody Bober

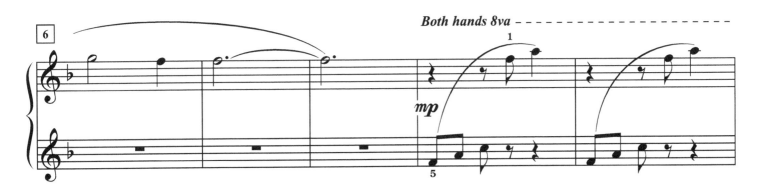

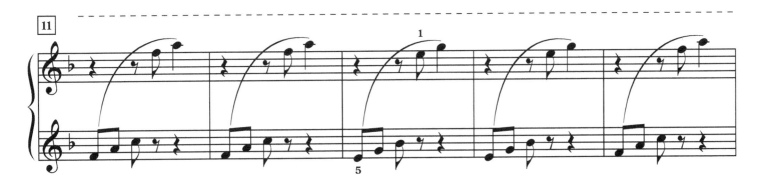

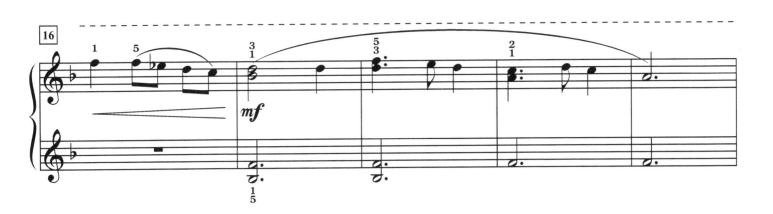

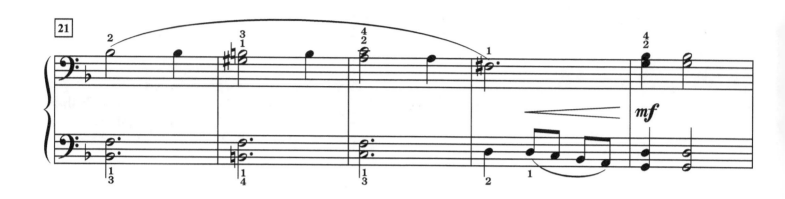

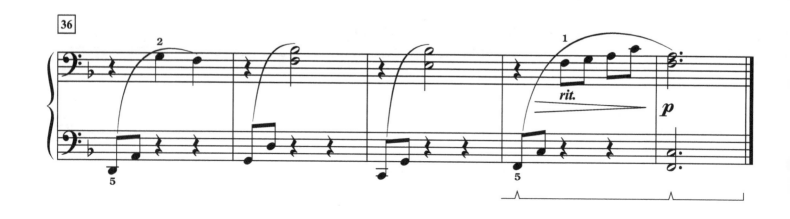

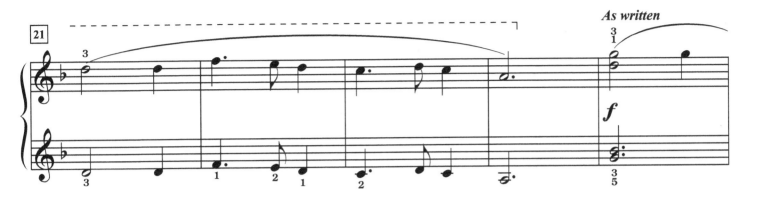

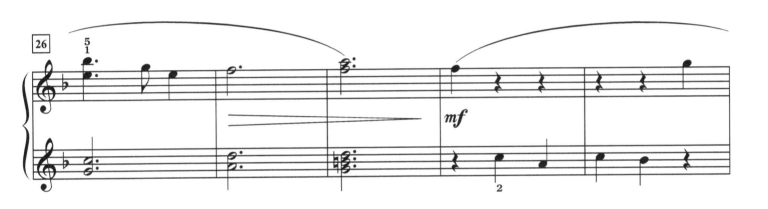

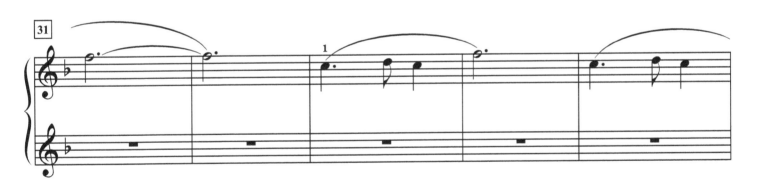

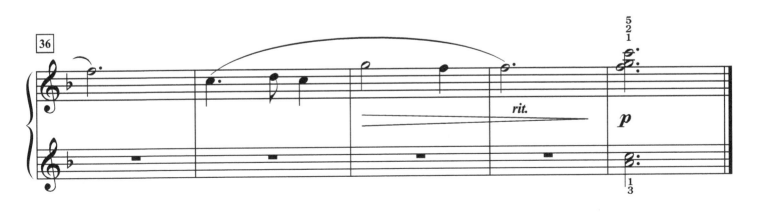

Go, Tell It on the Mountain

SECONDO

Traditional Spiritual
Arr. by Melody Bober

Go, Tell It on the Mountain

PRIMO

Traditional Spiritual
Arr. by Melody Bober

SECONDO

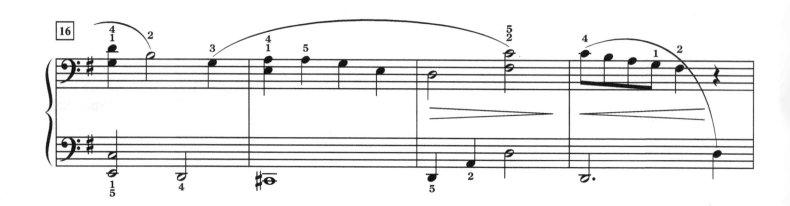

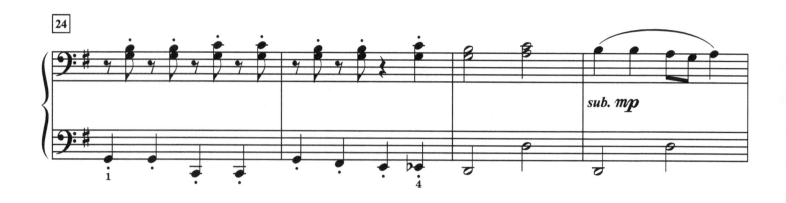

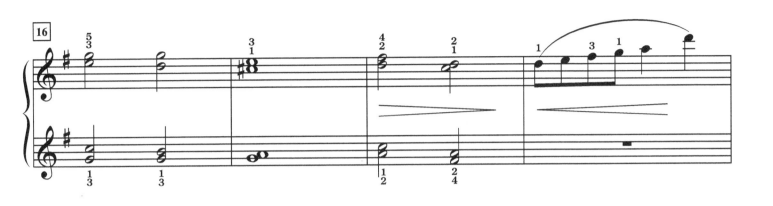

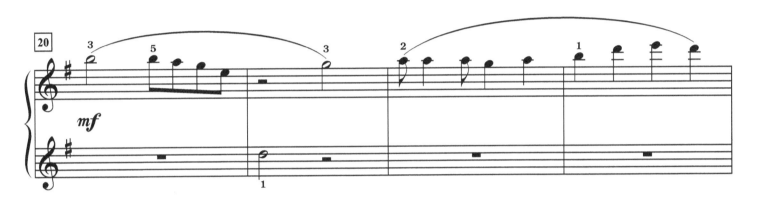

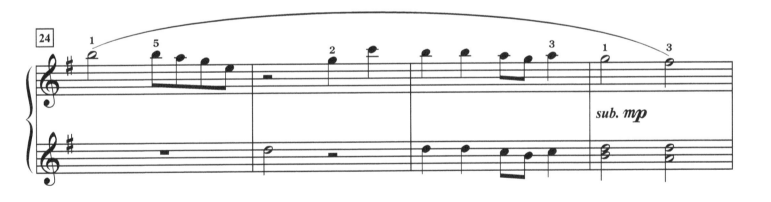

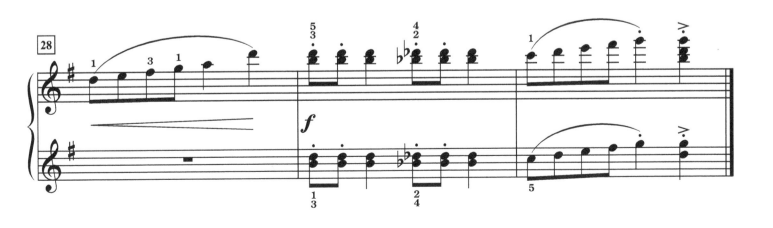

O Come, All Ye Faithful

SECONDO

John Francis Wade
Arr. by Melody Bober

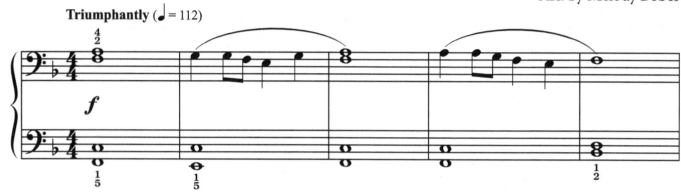

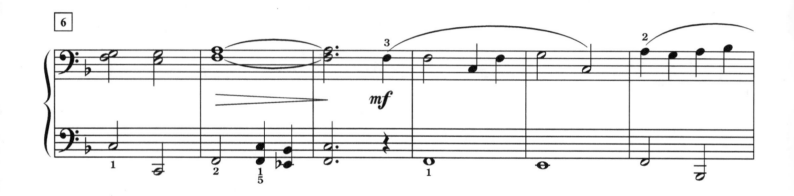

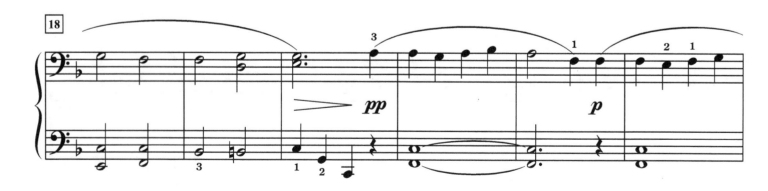

O Come, All Ye Faithful

PRIMO

John Francis Wade
Arr. by Melody Bober